COUPLES TRIVIA Q

Fun and Engaging Questions to Ask Before You Get Married or even After You are Married | Learn the Art of Mindful Connection and Intimacy in Marriage & Romantic Relationships

By

Bryan Bruce

MY GIFT TO YOU SCAN THE QR-CODE BELOW

LEGAL DISCLAIMER:

Any earnings or income statements, or earnings or income examples, are only estimates of what we think you could earn. There is no assurance you'll do as well. If you rely upon our figures, you must accept the risk of not doing as well. Where specific income figures are used and attributed to an individual or business, those persons or businesses have earned that amount. There is no assurance you'll do as well. If you rely upon our figures; you must accept the risk of not doing as well.

Any claims or representations, as to income earnings on this website, are not to be considered as average earnings. There can be no assurance that any prior successes, or past results, as to income earnings, can be used as an indication of your future success or results.

Monetary and income results are based on many factors. We have no way of knowing how well you will do, as we do not know you, your background, your work ethic, or your business skills or practices. Therefore, we do not guarantee or imply that you will win any incentives or prizes that may be offered, get rich, that you will do as well, or make any money at all. There is no assurance you'll do as well. If you rely upon our figures; you must accept the risk of not doing as well.

Internet businesses and earnings derived therefrom, have unknown risks involved and are not suitable for everyone. Making decisions based on any information presented in our products, services, or web site, should be done only with the knowledge that you could experience significant losses, or make no money at all.

All products and services by our company are for educational and informational purposes only. Use caution and seek the advice of qualified professionals. Check with your accountant, lawyer, or professional advisor, before acting on this or any information.

Users of our products, services, and web site are advised to do their due diligence when it comes to making business decisions, and all information, products, and services that have been provided should be independently verified by your qualified professionals. Our information, products, and services on this web site should be carefully considered and evaluated, before reaching a business decision, on whether to rely on them. All disclosures and disclaimers made herein or on our site, apply equally to any offers, prizes, or incentives, that may be made by our company.

You agree that our company is not responsible for the success or failure of your business decisions relating to any information presented by our company, or our company products or services.

INTRODUCTION

People crave intimacy and romance and that leaves a lot of folks asking **questions** about romantic relationships. All humans need to be loved and to love. But it is not an easy thing to do or find because love is not absolute. It is a living and nurturing relationship that is two-way: it ebbs and flows and can depend on how people treat each other.

People crave love and romantic relationships. Love is one of the most profound and most meaningful emotions known to man. Man's capacity to love and develop healthy relationships, however, does not always come naturally. Some people suffer from unhealthy or unloving relationships.

Some people have failed relationships because they did not give the conscious effort to make it flourish. Romantic relationships are some of the most difficult connections to cultivate and preserve – but it is not impossible to do so.

Every successful **romantic relationship** takes work – it needs the attention, care, commitment, and nurturing of two individuals who give to each other in a communally beneficial union.

This book discusses some of the most frequently asked questions about romantic relationships and offers answers, solutions, or advice about said questions.

One of the top questions about romantic relationships is this:

What are the cornerstones of a solid relationship?

Every relationship should have a solid foundation of **trust** and **respect**. Couples should be able to trust each other in all things – big and small. They should cultivate **honesty** and make it a commitment to be truthful to their partners. And that starts with knowing your partner and to that, you need to ask a lot of questions and have a lot of discussions.

It sounds so simple but it is a vital ingredient to the success of any relationship, romantic or otherwise. Additionally, couples should not only make it a point to care about each other and express that care, but they must also respect each other's needs and desires.

The succeeding questions about romantic relationships deal with many different aspects such as acceptance, communication, commitment, growing together, love languages, playfulness and intimacy, handling conflict, and reinforcing your relationship.

COMMUNICATION IN RELATIONSHIPS – THE CORNERSTONE OF A HEALTHY, FULFILLING RELATIONSHIP

Maintaining healthy communication in relationships may seem the easiest task in the world. However, communicating well and effectively is, much more often than not, the fruit of continued effort and care of both partners in a relationship.

It is the result of the realization of husband and wife in playing their parts, ensuring they can contribute the most for the success of their shared life.

Effective communication between husband and wife or any relationship for that matter can be easily neglected, due to a wide variety of reasons. In a romantic relationship, the result of this process can be seriously damaging, sometimes crippling it beyond repair.

These days, with our lives outside our homes, are growingly demanding and consuming in terms of time and energy, it is astonishingly easy to lose focus on communication.

This context makes it especially necessary to adopt an attitude that ensures that neither husband nor wife neglect communication in relationships. If they are to truly live happily ever after, both must work together on the relationship.

Communicating better can help both partners to become friends love more deeply and have a healthy respect for each other.

Having Better Communication in Relationships

There is a substantial difference between the act of talking or exchanging a few words and effective and productive communication within a relationship.

First things first, if you are determined to improve this part of your relationship with your better half, one of the things you should never deter from is being as honest as you can. When you need to talk about serious, important topics with your spouse, you should request the same honesty from him or her.

Otherwise, you´d just be wasting each other´s time and possibly creating new problems in your relationships, which is precisely what we are trying to avoid here.

Another thing to keep in mind is to be tolerant and available towards your spouse´s points of view, opinions, and solicitations or complaints. These are indispensable if you want to improve the way you understand each other. This is very essential to communication in relationships.

Try to show an interest, even if the talk you´re about to have isn´t particularly appealing to you. If your partner just needs you to listen to his/her worries, or simply get something out of his/her chest, even if it doesn´t concern your relationship directly; make a real effort to adopt a positive attitude.

If you disagree, you can always be honest and still be supportive and understanding. In the worst-case scenario, at least you showed you care. After all, you were listening.

Dealing with Time and Aggressiveness

A conversation between spouses should not be a contest, a fight to the death, or an attempt to simply establish whose blame it is, whatever the issue is. This attitude will help you prevent these things from happening as well, maintaining the levels of civility under control and avoiding excessive aggression from ruining your efforts to communicate better.

Another good strategy you can employ for better communication in relationships is to try to address any given issue with your spouse at the right time. In a certain sense, managing a relationship is also managing the past, a common history between two persons. Some people tend to accumulate concerns and regrets without really showing others how much importance these have for them.

Good communication should be fluid. Block it and pressure will grow. In a relationship, over the years, if you let these concerns and regrets pile up, if you constantly restrain from facing the bigger, most difficult issues, the results will probably be disastrous. And possibly lead to really violent outbursts.

On top of that, you will be constantly carrying around a heavy burden of blame towards your life partner.

This will not only be bad for you, as such levels of frustration can become unhealthy but most probably also have an effect on the way you treat your spouse. This could turn into yet another thing undermining the possibilities the both of you have to peacefully understand each other and settle your differences.

Simply try to address every issue as soon as you are conscious of it, as calmly and with the least amount of aggressiveness. Instead of running away from these conversations, why not face them, settle them and make room for merrier memories, thoughts, and emotions? This kind of attitude will certainly improve your communication in relationships.

Limiting the Distractions for Better Communication in Relationships

In times such as these, when our daily lives are stressful and demanding and the work hours incredibly consuming better communication in relationships is essential.

Also, we are in an age characterized by the proliferation of distractions, it is also critical to understand that effective communication requires quality time.

Turning off your gadgets, facing your spouse instead of the TV, being able to leave work outside the door are essential if you want to truly communicate. It can be hard and it may even require planning, but don´t forget to save a few hours, at least each week, to focus solely on your husband or wife.

Try your best to preserve that shared space where you can both be completely available for one another.

COUPLES CHALLENGE QUESTIONS

Do you want to know your spouse deeply? Then here are 23 couples challenge questions to help you get to know yourselves better and make you a better lover

You may have a wrong impression of your partner all because you have been dating for years. But if you have passed the stage of infatuation, these couples' challenge questions would help you.

It's a couple of challenge games that involves asking questions and answering. You may think you know everything about your partner once you've been dating for a few years. But almost always, what I've seen is that partners actually believe they know each other, but in reality, they just don't know their partner. They just assume they do.

Though the new relationship is always filled with a few white lies and many secrets. But as the relationships start to grow, both partners start to feel secure with each other, and the secrets start to come out in the open.

To truly experience the perfect relationship, you need to make each other feel comfortable, and you need to learn to think from your partner's perspective. And at times, the best way to find out your partner's perspective is by asking all the right questions. If your partner doesn't open up at first, ask your partner to question you first, hear your answer, and then answer.

If you don't know how to get your partner to open up, or how you can have the perfect relationship, use these 23 questions for couples. These 23 couples challenge questions would make strangers fall in love with each other and make you a better lover.

All these couples' challenge questions bring the couple closer together. Well, it's followed by four minutes of intense silence staring into each other's' eyes, to put it plainly:

Question 1: What is your goal in life? Have you achieved it?

Question 2: Can you tell me about yourself briefly?

Question 3: What do you value most in a friendship?

Question 4: How do you make good use of your time?

Question 5: What is your deepest fear?

Question 6: What makes you happy and satisfied in life?

Question 7: What is your treasured memory?

Question 8: How would you describe love?

Question 9: What gets you irritated towards the people?

Question 10: How would you describe an unselfish love?

Question 11: Can you tell me about your family?

Question 12: Are you closer to your mom than your dad?

Question 13: What was your childhood like?

Question 14: What qualities do I possess that got you attracted to me?

Question 15: Does it bother you if I don't keep appointments?

Question 16: What's the most embarrassing moment in your life?

Question 17: If there's one thing you'd want to change about me, what is it?

Question 18: How would you react to an expensive joke?

Question 19: If you were to die this evening with no opportunity to communicate with anyone, what would you most regret not having told someone? Why haven't you told them yet?

Question 20: Of all the people in your family, whose death would you find most disturbing? Why?

Question 21: Do you like sports? What kind of sports do you like?

Question 22: Do you like men who keep their armpits bushy?

Question 23: Why do you think some couples end up cheating on each other?

Couples who ask questions to get closer builds a perfect relationship. When communication is strong and the couple spends quality time with each other, it makes the relationship exciting and stronger.

All these couples challenge questions are also sort of relationship mind games which may be funny or a bit teasing but it all portraits a trait about your partner. It may allow you to know their view towards other people and insecurity or many other things.

Try to have a light-hearted conversation and ask each other these questions, and don't take offense no matter what. At the end of the day, your partner is opening up to you only because they feel secure. By getting angry or annoyed at any point, you're only going to make your partner hide deeper in their emotional shell.

What do you know about relationship mind games?

Relationship mind games are played by people who have little idea of how they continue to find themselves in a relationship. Though mind games are scary because of what surrounds us especially if we have been through a bad relationship before. But these mind games sometimes happen subconsciously.

Relationship mind games are another option for those who have few true intimacy skills. Because true intimacy is not always working well and with every person, the ability to participate in mind games is valid and necessary.

Therefore, learning this game can do you a world of good and a conversation game like this will allow you to connect and have fun in the process, even if the content of the talk is not that clever. You just have to have a playful mindset

Here are a few relationship mind games for couples to challenge themselves:

21 Questions:

This game is started in one conversation, and continued in the next, continuously like that until it reaches 21. It's a simple game, but when you start it, it becomes interesting because you would be so engrossed in asking many questions and before you know it, you've gone through all the 21 questions already.

I Have Never:

This game is daring because it involves drinks tea, juice or beer, etc. It's like you saying you have never done something before and your partner has done that same thing, then your partner has to take a sip from the drink. The beauty of this game consists in saying the things that you think your partner may have done and thus getting him to finish their drink first.

True or False:

In this game, you bring out a story or fact and allow your partner to contribute to it by asking if it's false or true and you discuss more on his/her choice.

If It Weren't for You:

This is another relationship game where the insecure or passive person who restricts his/her activities says the above words. The goal of the game is to **have fun** and you can stop the game at a certain point to discuss what you found interesting. And then go back to the game if you feel like it. Just be playful and don't take things too seriously.

Couples also have some 123 tag questions between themselves. These 123-couple tag **questions** are played when you and your partner count 123 to answer a question at the same time. Such question could be:

- Which of the celebrities do you want as a boyfriend/girlfriend?
- Do you watch movies? What is your favorite movie then?
- What if there is a fire outbreak in your building and your girlfriend/boyfriend is ill to stand up and you also have some valuables to take out, what will you do?
- What sentence or phrase do you repeat most?

Also, there are a couple's challenge retreats that allow the couple a respite from the cares they have every week and make them get a better view of themselves. Not only is the couples challenge retreat fun but it's the way the activities are related to real-life which is amazing and makes you think about some important decisions.

The couples challenge questions will help you to create value in your relationship and impress on you both the importance of communication and helps to bring you couples together.

You can also create your couple's challenge ideas or games with a little imagination. The point is to connect on a deeper level and create a lasting bond between you two.

QUESTIONS ABOUT MARRIAGE

Marriage is a thing of beauty but sometimes scary; hence couples ask questions about marriage just before they walk down the aisle. Statistical data may disagree, but those who base their relationship on mutual honesty, trust, and love are the happiest people on the planet.

Though no one knows what the future holds for them, some people still yearn for the promise of love to each other for the rest of their lives. It gives them the inspiration and courage to accomplish anything they want.

You may be sure they'll keep their promise but, at the same time, your partner is might want a big bachelor party or a nice ring. But it takes a lot more than a big party, a nice ring, and signing a piece of paper to truly give oneself to another person.

Marriage should be based on more than blind trust. If you're serious about tying the knot – make sure of your future partner's **honesty** and dedication. You can only be so sure about how authentic someone is, but you need to try assessing your chances for a successful marriage as much as possible.

As a starting point, make sure their answers to the below questions about marriage satisfy you, and above all that they respond to these questions with a heart.

- *What do you love about me?*
  Everyone should know and think often about the exact reasons they love. Even if these reasons are selfish, they should be apparent and not circumstantial. You love someone for what they do for you and how the things they do make you feel, not for the fact that they're tall or rich or left-handed.

Everyone has a slightly different answer to this question, but someone who hasn't articulated their answer to it (at least in their mind) is most likely under the initial spell of intense emotion. If he/she can't explain why he or she loves you, then why would you be certain about spending the rest of your days with them?

- *How do you see the rest of your life with me?*
  Marriage is supposed to be a life-long journey. But unfortunately, most marriages end at the nearest crossroads. Not sharing certain personal goals and dreams is one thing, but wanting to lead completely different ways of life is another entirely.

This is one of the few questions about marriage that is overlooked by almost everyone. "Opposites attract" is a saying that works with small details – not major life-choices.

Your future partner must be able to give at least a dozen reasons and examples of long-term experiences he/she will share with you. 65 percent of all marriages wouldn't end in divorce if everyone answered this question honestly before taking such a huge leap.

- *What steps will you be willing to take to keep the romance alive?*
  Maintaining the authenticity of real romance is not easy after the initial few years. It's a psychological issue, but just thinking about the other person is not enough.

It takes real effort and lots of creativity. Your partner should not just be able to continuously impress you and make you proud – they should want to do so.
The emotional component of your love life won't be able to survive for long. This is normal.

Most people are past that point by the time they even enter marriage. Both of you need to know how to constantly try to encourage romantic love with each other.

- ***Will you stick with me, no matter where life takes you?***
  You never know exactly where your life will take you and what it'll teach you. Along the way, people can become someone they never were before. You and your husband/wife must take time to make numerous conscious efforts to stick together and not let work or personal interests drive you apart.

Another major reason most marriages end up as failing relationships is that people view getting married as a final goal. People think that they've already accomplished everything they could in the relationship when the truth is that marriage isn't the end of anything – it's just the beginning.

Additionally, while enjoying the good times together is also important, going through the hard times can make or break a marriage. If you or your partner isn't ready for it, know that there will come a point in your relationship when you will have to decide whether you'll be there for each other even though being alone would make you better off.

- ***Are you willing to admit when you're wrong and be considerate of my opinions?***
  A vitally important relationship skill is being able to control one's ego. Being competitive is just fine in most situations and is even a good thing in some, but marriage is not one of them.

Can you respect your partner enough to admit you're wrong? Can they do the same, without holding grudges?
The thing about arguments is that they often don't have a

clear solution. People tend to argue over opinion rather than fact. Since an opinion can't be right or wrong, you need to be able to let things go – agree to disagree

- *Will you commit to being a good parent to our future kids?*
  Sure, your partner can't know that they will be a great parent, but you'll know how much effort they intend to put into becoming one depending on their answer.

This is one of the few questions about marriage that should be asked without prior warning. Is your future wife/husband even thinking about kids? Do they feel sure about the fact that they'll have kids with you?

If both of you are on the same page, you'll feel the enthusiasm with which they answer. And though, in reality, no one can be sure – they can decide to give it their best shot.

- *If things go downhill for me, will you be there to support me not just financially, but also mentally and physically?*
  Unfortunately, life is bound to bring some measure of bad news. Unexpected circumstances can leave you unable to support yourself financially, they may make you depressed or even physically damaged.

Does your partner love you enough to be ready for that? Will they be your therapist? Will he or she take some weight off your shoulders if you can't carry it on your own?

- *Will you promise to maintain your lifestyle and not let go of your personal goals?*
  Just because marriage is the beginning of something new, doesn't make it the end of anything. That being said, any serious relationship will surely transform your lifestyle – it just won't change what you want from life.

The perception that marriage replaces all other goals and ambitions a person has is a rumor based on the unsuccessful majority. The truth is that allowing each other to have room for personal growth is a huge stepping stone of a great relationship.

You fell in love with each other because of who you each were before you got married, so you need to make sure you don't let yourselves go.

Are you both ready to continue taking care of your physical well-being by staying healthy and exercising at least as much as you do now? Will you get check-ups and take supplemental vitamins to make sure you stay healthy?

If these questions about marriage seem shallow or plain silly to you, just think about the strain health problems can put upon families. Having a seriously ill partner can create huge problems for both of you.

QUESTIONS FOR COUPLES GAME

Questions for couples' games are questions that couples need, whether at the early stages of a relationship or later into the relationship. It could also serve those who are introverts in so many ways.

For people just starting a relationship, it's not that hard to talk amongst each other. You just met someone new and the excitement is there and you want to get to know him/her right away. But of course, this initial curiosity will only serve to know the person on the surface and not that deep.

Knowing someone deeply requires time and commitment and loads of interest in the person. Unfortunately, these qualities seem to be lacking for a fresh relationship except in some cases.

But also, there is the danger that as the relationship progresses into weeks and months, you two might find it hard to sustain that initial excitement. This is even made worse if both partners have demanding jobs or other things that keep people busy.

At this stage, talking and paying attention to your spouse will be an effort; one that you both need to make if you two want to keep the relationship going. Hence questions for couples' games.

Questions for couples' games will sound so amusing if both partners will approach likewise. The thing here is to make your relationship fun and interesting. You both will have the opportunity to laugh and learn just how compatible you are as new couples. And for the older couples, it will help bring you both closer than before and remind you of how excited you both were when you met.

Most of the questions for couples' games may not be related to relationships but it will help you understand why your partner might have changed since you met him/her and their new way of thinking and seeing issues.

Like it or not, couples, married or just dating will change. But that doesn't mean that the relations or marriage will come to end. That's these questions for couples' games will help you to keep learning about each other and growing together.

Questions for couples' game-For the Husband

1- What blessing that your life partner issued you came true with the greatest astonishment?

2- Between you and your partner; who would you say likes to save and who is a spindrift?

3- Who does your wife chat with on the phone the most?

4- Which one of your wife's friends would look best in a two-piece?

5- On the off chance that your wife could pick one thing of yours to dispose of, what would that be?

6- At the point when your wife says, 'hey sweetie, they're playing our tune' what music would that be?

7- What living superstar lady will your wife say she most appreciates?

8- What color are your wife's most loved shoes?

9- Who talked about marriage first, you or your wife?

10- Your wife is held up at the dentist's office. Which magazine will she read? Logical American, Good Housekeeping, People, Field and Stream, Fabulousness?

11- Assuming that you told your wife that tomorrow you would do any one thing from her To-Do list, what might she pick?

12- When did you last give your wife flowers?

13- What was the breed and name of her pet when she was small?

14- What is the most she has ever paid for a couple of shoes?

15- What is your spouse's favorite color?

16- What was the last book spouse read?

17- How will your spouse react to an inconvenience?

18- Who is the better cook?

19- Assuming that you and your spouse were to go get another puppy, what pooch would he need to get?

QUESTIONS FOR COUPLES
GAME- FOR THE WIFE

1- Is your car back, front, or all-wheel drive? What will she say it is?

2- What is the most surprising gift your mate has ever purchased for you?

3- What might your spouse say was the exact opposite thing you two argue about?

4- What rate of the housework would your partner say they do?

5- When was the last time you and your spouse had a long hard kiss?

6- What piece of clothing does your partner wear that you just can't stand?

7- What is your partner's most annoying habit?

8- What is the most beautiful gift your partner has ever bought for you?

9- What is the vacation destination that your spouse would in all probability pick for an impromptu vacation?

10- Who takes more time to get dressed? You or your partner?

11- When your wife was 13 years of age, what would she have liked to be when she grew up?

12- Who do you believe is quicker witted or has the higher IQ – you or your life partner?

13- What is your life partner's most used swear word or swear word?

14- Assuming that your spouse could be any popular individual, living or dead, who might that be?

15- What is the one thing that your spouse accomplishes for

you that he/she despises but goes along with it just because you like it?

16- On the off chance that your life partner could wear one dress of yours, what might that be?

17- What color was the front door of the first house you lived in?

18- Assuming that you had $100 you could spend on anything you needed, what would your spouse agree that you buy?

20- Assuming that you could have consistent access to one store, what store would it be?

21- What is your life partner's top pick "comfort or nourishment"?

22- What one piece of clothing does the spouse wear that you just can't stand?

23- Who might your mate say be the "better catch" out of you two?

24- What might your mate say his/ her most prominent quality would be?

25- What interesting or humiliating thing about your mate does everybody know about?

26- What interesting or humiliating thing about your mate does your mate thinks nobody knows?

27- What is your mate's most annoying habit?

28- How many pairs of shoes do you have that are not in a storage room at this time?

29- Other than the day of your wedding or the conception of any of your kids, what one day of your marriage might you most want to experience once more?

30- Assuming that you needed to change occupations with one of your friends, who might you pick?

31- What is your spouse's most loved food?

32- What will your spouse say is your most loved food?

QUESTIONS TO ASK A COUPLE
FOR BETTER CONNECTION

Occasionally it is always nice to conduct a sort of health check on a relationship, just to obtain a better understanding of the state of one's marriage and the state of fulfillment and contentment in the marriage.

When one neglects to check on the state of their relationship, problems begin to arise and one may come to the realization that the state of affairs in the marriage is not what it used to be.

For you to promote and maintain a sort of closeness and connection in marriage while making sure that you are together in a relationship with the right person, and just being together because you have no choice, then you should stop and reflect on the reason why you are in the relationship at all and whether you are still doing the right thing

Listed below you will find numerous questions to ask a couple, questions to ask your spouse, or even questions to ask yourself all to better understand the nature of your relationship.

A Generalized Question to Ask A Couple Could Be Conducted as Follows

Are You Two Always Fighting and Arguing With Each Other?

If this is happening more often than it's supposed to, then it's time to find out what the real problem is. So, by following the related series of questions you may be able to obtain a better understanding of the state of your marriage and your happiness and fulfillment in life.

It is important to address this issue or conflict before it evolves into an even bigger problem. Leaving problems or issues unaddressed can eventually contribute to bad feelings and stone-walling your partner and a loss of empathy and compassion towards one another.

Another question to ask a couple that you should consider is-

Do you feel that your spouse takes their job more seriously than you?

The moment one does not feel a sense of self-worth or importance being with their partner, the person's outlook will surely change towards their partner. This will lead to the partner looking for other ways to fulfill themselves and be accepted.

Often these methods will lead to complications and more problems rather than solve the underlying issues within the marriage. To prevent this misplacement of priorities you would be better off talking things over with your partner. Let him or she understand how you feel because chances are, they might understand that there is a problem.

It is important to establish compromises and let tensions die down if it has gotten up to that stage so that both members in the marriage regain their sense of self-worth.

Nobody would like to be just ignored; you also need to look a bit deeper to see if you will need to be more patient and understanding.

Have You Lost All Sense of Being in The Present?

Do you feel like you are missing something and asking yourself, is this all there is? Is this going to be your lot in life?

There is no doubt that moods change, feelings change, and more so with the ladies as they experience fluctuations in hormones, but then she should watch to make sure that the mood changes are not becoming a permanent state of being for her. The same goes for the guy.

Both parties are in this for the long term and both should make the effort to see that any issue that arises is tackled before it gets out of hand. To this, both partners should add fun and laughter into their lives as much as possible.

A question to consider about each individual in the marriage could be-

Are Forcing Yourself to Remain Invisible Just to Keep the Relationship?

There is no better place to be yourself except with the one that you love and cherish. If you can't be yourself in a relationship then there is a problem. A relationship is meant to be non-judgmental and no partner should force the other to be what they don't want to be.

You both should accept each other's goods and as well as the faults unless the faults are just simply something that you can't ignore like an abusive spouse. And such an abusive spouse should not expect the rule of loving someone for who they are to apply to them in this case.

Do you find yourself stuck in a relationship you don't like simply because you are afraid to go out into the world alone?

It happens all the time, and more with the ladies than the guys. You see grown adults so petrified of being alone that they force themselves to endure heartbreaking situations in a relation and let themselves be abused countless times.

That fear is just something they have created in their heads and minds that are not real at all. The only solution to that is for such people to be brave and take that leap of faith.

No matter where you are, it can never be a bed of roses all the time, so you just might as well accept it and move and deal with issues as them at you with or without your partner. You have a life to live and interests to pursue so go out there and make this happen, don't just stand there while life passes you by.

Another Question to Ask A Couple Could Also Be-

Are you under the impression that your spouse ignores you emotionally completely?

This is one question that is easy for couples to be guilty of especially couples that hardly talk to each other. Supporting each other emotionally is very important even when the other person doesn't have the solution at hand or have a clue what to do.

Take it any way you like, but it always takes two to tango, and when issues such as emotional resentment arise, the discussion will be your best out of it.

You and your partner could decide to do something crazy and a list of what each person will do for the other to support them emotionally that way the stalemate will be broken and restore your relationship to a much better footing.

QUESTIONS ABOUT RELATIONSHIPS ALL COUPLES NEEDS TO ANSWER

The following are questions about relationships that every couple will need to address at some point in their life.

If you are in a committed relationship or starting a new one these **questions** will help you determine whether this particular relationship is going in the right direction or maybe you should put the brakes on things and wait until the outstanding issues are addressed.

By following these tips, you will be in a position to make the most of your relationship.

1) Do You Trust Each Other Completely?

When it comes to questions about relationships, if there is no **trus**t then everything else does not matter. You need to know whether the person you are with will stick with you through thick and thin without betraying you. This is not an easy question to answer but you need to be 100% honest with yourself or it could lead to serious unhappiness in the future.

2) When Did You Last Say "I Love You" To Each Other And Mean It?

Another question that has to be addressed when it comes to questions about relationships is how openly affectionate are you with one another. Simple things like saying "I love you' can put your partner at ease and make them happy but if you or they are not saying it often or meaning it when they say it then it could be a sign that there are some issues to work out.

3) Is the Overall Level of Intimacy Acceptable?

Each person has their own desired level of intimacy; some people like it often while others don't like it as much. There are no absolute right or wrong answers but if you or your partner feels like their needs are not being met then this is something that has to be discussed and addressed before resentment begins to form.

4) Do You Laugh Together Often?

Comedy is a great way to reduce stress and enjoy life but if you and your partner are not able to share laughs then it is a sign that something is wrong with the relationship, everyone has to laugh it is just part of being a normal human being so if you and your spouse are not laughing then it is time to have a serious conversation ASAP.

5) Do You Smile Whenever You Think of Your Partner?

Do you remember when the two of you **fell in love** together and how wonderful it was? If you still smile whenever you think about your partner then that is a sign that the relationship looks promising however this is just one item out of many to address when working through the various questions about relationships.

6) Have You Ever Thought About Cheating on Your Significant Other?

This is a question that every couple needs to face and one of the most important questions about relationships that people need to address. While some people flirt if you have seriously thought about being intimate with another person or your partner that should be treated as a serious red flag and dealt with immediately or you could be going down the path of infidelity.

7) Do You See A Long-Term Relationship with Your Partner?

This is one question that every couple will need to address at some point and very important when it comes to questions about relationships. This one ranks in the top. If you cannot see a future with the person you are with then there is no point in continuing the relationship from this point forward.

8) Are the Two of Your Best Friends?

The most successful relationships are those where both the man and woman feel like lovers and best friends at the same time. If there is a feeling of closeness between both the man and woman simultaneously then this is a clear indication that the relationship is going well.

9) Can You Imagine Your Life Without Your Partner?

This is the biggest question to address in the questions about the relationships segment. While we all have bad days where we bicker and fight from time to time however can you imagine life without your partner and if so, how would it feel? This is a question that is painful for some. If you cannot imagine living without your partner then you have found your "soulmate" if you believe in that term.

10) Do You Like Your In-laws?

Do you like your in-laws and does your partner feel the same way about your family? When you marry a person you also marry their family in a sense so you need to look at their family as well, do you get along. While not every family is perfect you need to find a happy medium for both you and your spouse if you want to make the most of your relationship and enjoy all it has to offer.

It is not always easy to find harmony between two families but it is possible and when done right it can make the relationship stronger. While the **relationship questions** we have just covered may seem intrusive and difficult they are necessary if you want to know whether your relationship is stable or should you move on to another person. The sooner these questions are addressed the happier you can be so be sure to get them answered ASAP.

BEGINNERS RELATIONSHIP QUESTIONS

If you would like to read up some more on Questions About Relationships, then check out the links below, and don't forget to show some love by sharing this article.

A relationship is hard, I know, I've been there. It's a complicated thing and many people have relationship questions they want answers to despite all the books and sites dedicated to relationships.

Many people just jump into a relationship, not thinking about any consequences or without any real plans. Now, I'm not saying that you should have a plan laid out in front of you on your first date, love is unpredictable.

I'm just saying that you should get to know each other from day one.

And that's what this list is for, to get to know each other so that both of you know what you're heading into.

So here they are, in no particular order, 35 relationship questions a couple should ask each other in the beginning, so that they may enjoy a beautiful and healthy relationship for as long as possible.

Oh, and by the way, I'm not implying that all of these should be asked nor answered on the first date, or first three. I'm just saying that over time, try to check these questions off your relationship bucket list.

Relationship Questions-Beginners

1. Are you a jealous person by nature?

2. Have you ever been sacked from a job?

3. Did you have a decent childhood?

4. Did you have a rough childhood?

5. What are your hobbies? Your interests?

6. What kind of education do you have?

7. What kind of music do you like? Favorite band, singer?

8. What's your favorite meal?

9. What kind of food do you like?

10. What's your favorite color?

11. What do you like in a man or woman?

12. Have you ever been to a country other than your own?

13. Have you ever been a player? That has slept around a lot?

14. What do you do for a living?

15. Do you live alone, with someone or with a room-mate?

16. Where do you live?

17. Are you a cat or dog person?

18. Have you ever been to Europe?

19. Have you ever truly hated someone in your life? If yes, what did he/she/they do to earn your hatred?

20. Have you ever truly loved another person besides your family?

21. Have you ever been in a serious relationship?

22. Are you a night person or an early riser?

23. Do you enjoy coffee? Or are you more of a tea person?

24. Do you enjoy the video and computer games?

25. Are you a party person or more of a stay-in kind of person?

26. Have you ever tried drugs? If yes, what kind?

27. Do you drink a lot?

28. Do you smoke? If yes, then for how long? Have you ever tried to quit?

29. Have you ever lashed out at your parents in your teen years?

30. How are your parents? Ice-cold or welcoming?

31. When did you lose your virginity? Assuming you did?

32. Have you ever won anything in any kind of competition or lottery?

33. Have you ever gotten into a fight before? What led to this fight?

34. Do you own a pet? If so, what kind and race?

35. Do you have kids?

RELATIONSHIP QUESTIONS-
THE VETERAN RANKS

Now that we've gotten past a bunch of related questions you might want to ask your partner at the beginning of your relationship, here's a different one coming right at you.

This one is for the veteran couples, maybe for those who have lost their spark and want to reignite it again.

Or perhaps it's for those who just want to see if they truly know their partner. In any case, it's a fun exercise for any kind of couple with a few years under their belt.

Here they are, 35 relationship questions a veteran couple should ask each other!

1. Do you still like me as a person?
2. What am I doing wrong in your eyes?
3. What do you want me to do to make things better?
4. How have these years been in your eyes?
5. Is there anything I would've done better or differently?
6. Do you want kids?
7. Are you cheating on me? Have you ever cheated?
8. Do you want to stay with me from now on as well?
9. What can we do to make things better?
10. Are you bored with this relationship?
11. Should we party more?
12. Do you miss your old life? Enough to leave us behind?
13. Have you ever thought about leaving me or us?
14. What's your most treasured moment in this relationship?
15. What's your worst moment?
16. Do you have any regrets about us and our past?

17. Have you ever dreamed your life will be different from what it is now?

18. Do you want to be with your friends more?

19. Do you enjoy the company of your friends more than I?

20. Do you still truly love me?

21. Do you feel like changing something in our lives?

22. Do you like the place we live in?

23. Do you want to move to another town or house?

24. Do you enjoy your job?

25. Have you ever lied to me?

26. Have you ever kept something from me, looking out for my best interest?

27. Have you ever loved or liked someone else during our relationship?

28. Have you ever thought about doing something I wouldn't enjoy?

29. Do you like my parents?

30. Does your parents like me?

31. Have you ever talked about me behind my back?

32. Have you ever complained about me?

33. Have you ever praised me?

34. Have you ever thought about our relationship and thought that it's the best thing in the world?

35. Do you want to leave me?

Okay, I know that many of these relationship questions may sound a little depressing, but trust me, it's for the greater good of your relationship and your future as a couple.

The trick to this is to be 100 % honest with each other.

Why lie?

Just tell the truth and if your partner truly loves you then he or she will understand (unless you've done something truly horrific and destroyed everything you and your partner stand for) and keep on loving you.

Now as I said in the beginning, relationships are hard.

It's so hard that none of these relationship questions might even help you find any clarity in your life. The key to having a healthy relationship is simply by being honest with each other and respecting one another.

Betraying either of those principles is a recipe for marital and relationship disaster, believe me, I know how it feels.

FUN ROMANTIC QUESTIONS FOR COUPLES

One of the best ways to break the ice when dating someone and after the first few dates or even after a while of dating is to ask romantic questions. They can help make your partner feel closer to you and they can help you both learn about each other's likes and dislikes.

Some of these romantic questions for couples may push your boundaries as a couple but make sure to understand before asking each other these questions that they are meant to be fun and to provide you with meaningful conversations. Use these as a way to get to know each other.

Both parties should be open-minded enough to give honest answers and not be judged by the other, hence the consent to it together.

What Is the One Secret That You Are Too Afraid to Tell Me?

No matter what stage you are in a relationship couples usually have one or two secrets from their previous relationships that they are too afraid to tell their current partner. If you ask this question then the two of you don't have to worry about your secrets anymore. There is nothing more romantic than not having secrets from each other.

How Would You Describe Love?

This is one of the best romantic questions for couples to ask before you say the big three words. If you ask this question sometime before you say them you can ensure that you won't say "I love you" too early. No matter how long you have been a couple this is a great question.

What Do I Do That Turns You Off?

Related to the question above you should ask this one so that you can nip any bad habits in the bud. If you are doing something that turns your partner off chances are that you are upsetting them without you even knowing that. Asking this question can help improve your relationship and even save it if you are on the rocks.

Do You Get Jealous When I Look at Other People?

Let's face it, most people have wandering eyes. Just because we look at other people doesn't mean we like them in the same way that we like our partners. Use this as a conversation starter and to let your significant other know that you love them more than anyone else.

What Do You Think of Public Displays of Affection?

Public displays of affection can be anything from holding hands in public to going at it in public. It is important to find what your partner is comfortable doing in public and do not exceed that unless they agree to push their limits.

What Do You Think Is the Most Romantic Song?

Not all couples like the same music and not all couples think the same songs are romantic. Ask this question to help find out what songs you should play when it comes time to "have a laundry" as people have started to call it so that they don't ruin young ears.

Which of My Outfits Do You Like the Most?

This is a great question to find out what your partner likes to see you in. It can also help you gauge how other people see you. Need to know the perfect outfit for next week's date? Don't forget to ask this question then. By the way, answering your birthday suit may seem humorous and it may be true but it won't help your partner decide what to wear in most cases.

What Would You Like Me to Do More Of?

Everyone likes when their significant other does something for them. This could be as simple as holding your partner's hand more often or it could get into something more graphic. Ask this question to make sure you are pleasing your significant other to the fullest potential.

These romantic questions for couples are great starts for conversations and to get to know your partner, their likes, and their dislikes. They also help to build trust, respect, and friendship in relationships.

Use your best judgment when asking them as some of them may not be appropriate for all scenarios. Take away all seriousness, laugh, and have some fun. Answer all of the questions honestly and tell your partner to do the same otherwise the game is not as fun and you are wasting your time.

WOULD YOU RATHER QUESTIONS FOR COUPLES

Are you looking for a good way to get to know your significant other while having fun? Would you rather questions are always a great way to do this. You take turns asking each other questions that start with "Would you rather". Sometimes the hard part with this game is thinking up the questions so we have come up with a list of great would you rather questions for couples.

Would you rather go on a date or stay in?

This is one of the best would you rather question to help you start getting some dating ideas. After a few dates, it can be trying to come up with a way to spice it up. Imagine further down the road it is even harder. Improve your relationship with this "would you rather questions".

Would you rather kiss on the first date or not?

Yes, you are already dating but this question can still tell you about your partner. This will show you how your partner acted on your first date versus what they would have preferred. Sometimes they don't match up, if they don't this may be a topic for conversation down the road.

Would you rather kiss me or wait for me to take the imitative?

This question may seem obvious to the people who think that it is always the man's job to take the imitative but this is a new world. Take turns asking your partner this question and their answer may surprise you. It's also great for those rare couples who haven't kissed yet to break out.

Would you rather be friends with my ex or hate them?

This is a good question to ask if you want to know whether you should keep your exes a secret. If your partner says they hate them it is probably a good idea to not mention them unless completely unavoidable. Some people want to hear about their partner's exes as weird as that sounds.

Would you rather live in the city or the country?

This question may seem obvious by where someone lives but people don't always live where they want to. Sometimes work keeps you living somewhere else. This would you rather question helps you learn about your partner's likes and helps you determine if you want the same things.

Would you rather be hated or forgotten?

Part fun part learning, this question will help you determine whether your significant other places a high amount of value on what other people think of them. Sometimes this will surprise you.

Would you rather choose truth or dare?

This is a good question to help you probe how daring your partner is. Those who pick truth may be less daring. Just a heads up this isn't always true; it's just a good way to start gauging. Maybe you will learn that it is time that you guys start taking more risks or start throttling back a little bit.

Would you rather make a lot of money or enjoy your work?

With this question, you can determine whether or not your significant other prefers objects or life experiences. If they prefer objects, well hopefully they don't think you are an object. Also, be sure to consider other factors. Your partner may be trying to earn that money for you or maybe they have loans to pay off.

Would you rather have love or a great career?

Another one of possibly world-shattering would you rather questions. This can help you determine where your partner's ambitions lay. Do you want to stay with someone who would break up with you for the perfect job? Probably not.

While thinking of would you rather questions can be a hard task, it can also be hard to answer the questions. Many people are shy, especially when it comes to answering difficult questions in front of their partner. Talk with your partner before the game and come to an agreement that it is a game and you will not get mad at each other. Play honestly and have fun.

QUESTIONS FOR COUPLES TO KEEP YOU AND YOUR PARTNER ON YOUR TOES

No don't get all worked up for anything, I didn't mean that to sound anyway negative. These questions are meant for you both to enjoy yourselves and have some fun.

I frequently see and hear couples searching for good things to ask their sweetheart or things to do. There may be a lot of reasons, what is yours?

Looking for ways to get to know your partner even more?

Using up conversation ideas in your head for a date with your partner?

First date nerves and don't know what to discuss?

Indeed, here are the first of 100 questions for couples out as many as you think up that can break the ice and get a discussion going.

What's more, remember that the most critical thing is to have a ton of fun! Even though this may appear to be anything but fun to sit and rundown all the 100 questions for couples before with your girlfriend/boyfriend; just pick one or two and discuss it together deeply.

So, make jocks with them, can laugh at yourselves, and discuss them, talk about the answers, appreciate the discussion and try to enjoy each other's company

You might be surprised by just how much you both don't know each other anymore even after being together for a while.

Heck, this happens to married couples, people who have spent years together.

All of a sudden, they no longer know each other. But with these 100 questions for couples, you will be able to get the fire burning again and you will start to feel that sweet tingling sensation at the pit of your Tommy again.

There is nothing wrong in wooing your partner all of again guys, believe me, she would love you even more for that.

Remember that you have to agree with your partner and make the conscious choice to enjoy the whole thing because some questions might make get one party upset or go defensive. Just be aware that this is a "no judgment" time for you both.

Even as hard as it might seem to go through them; you might be surprised that after things have calmed down that the bond between you two will grow stronger, richer, and better than before.

So here we go;

1. What was your best occupation?

2. What was your worst job so far?

3. Let me know all the places you worked

4. Tell me what you know about your closest friend

5. Let me know about your family

6. Let me know about your relatives

7. What was your first Car?

8. Most favorite movie star?

9. Most loved performer?

10. Favourite Song?

11. What were your extraordinary minutes?

12. What was your first girlfriend/boyfriend like?

13. Did you like your first kiss?

14. What is the most idiotic thing you have ever done?

15. Have you ever been captured?

16. Political alliance?

17. Have you voted in favor of somebody you wished you hadn't?

18. Have you utilized Drugs?

19. Do you like to shop?

20. What is your most ideal approach to relaxation?

21. What's the most loving thing would like to do alone?

22. Have you ever had a one night stand?

23. How would you describe love?

24. What's the most erotic thing a guy and a girl can do

together?

25. On the off chance that you discovered a $100 what might you do?

26. Do you want kids/more children?

27. Is it safe to say that you are a decent parent?

28. What makes a decent parent?

29. Is it safe to say that you are romantic?

30. How could we make our life more exciting?

31. Which do you like most, cat or dog?

32. Did you have pets growing up?

33. Do like sleeping naked?

34. What are your most loved midnight snacks?

35. Do you work out?

36. If I called you a horny pervert, how would you confront my accusation?

37. Have you ever snooped on me behind my back?

38. What is one food you will never stop eating?

39. What food can you not live without?

40. What's your most loved drink?

41. What's a flawless day?

42. What CDs have you ever listened to?

43. What number of DVDs have you ever watched?

44. What's the most loved thing to burn your cash on?

45. What is the most unusual thing about you?

46. What's always on your bedside table?

47. Is it safe to say that you are shoddy or thrifty?

48. Ever been enamored with two people at the same time?

49. How were your evaluations in secondary school?

50. Who is your most loved teacher?

51. Do have any relatives in prison?

52. Do you like pizza?

53. What you like best, dark or white?

54. Is a Glass half-full or half-empty?

55. Ever been to a nourishment rack?

56. Have you ever milked a cow?

57. Ever tipped a cow?

58. Bath or shower?

59. Mountains or the shoreline?

60. Which do you prefer, planes or cars?

61. Most loved unsurpassed film?

62. Most awful film you have ever seen?

63. Best show you have been to?

64. Beer, wine, or coffee?

65. What's the best vacation you have ever had?

66. If you could resign tomorrow what might you do?

67. What's the most awful vacation?

68. Three spots you would love to visit?

69. What if I told you I don't want children?

70. If you could do anything that might it be?

71. Superpowers you wish you had?

72. Ever had a massage?

73. Perfect romantic dinner?

74. How many times do like having a vacation in a year?

75. Where did you discover cash when you were level destitute?

76. What do like thinking of when you are alone and meditating?

77. Tell me something about your youth; one you haven't told me yet?

78. Ever hit a jackpot on a slot machine?

79. Have you ever won the lottery?

80. What might you do with your lottery rewards?

81. Is it safe to say that you are a slick bastard?

82. Can't stand being around individuals who_____?

83.Which do you like best crowds or small gatherings?

84. How long would you like to live?

85. If you were to keep one which would you prefer, your sight or hearing?

86. Ever really liked anyone who you never met before?

87. Outstanding irritations?

88. What irritates you the most?

89. What is the sweetest surprise you have ever received?

90. Real mood killers?

91. Do you like Tattoos?

92. Body painting?

93. Do you like body piercings?

94. Would you like to have plastic surgery?

95. Do you like computer geeks?

96. Do you like being active?

97. Would you like to learn how to play an instrument?

98. Have you been in a band before?

99. What are your most humiliating minute?

100. Would you like to go to a Nude beach?

These 100 questions for couples will you both to think about specific topics and understand each other's point of view at the same grow closer together. They will draw you both out and understand each other's wants, desires, and aspirations.

Remember, there are two major objectives here, know each other better and have some fun.

CONVERSATION STARTERS FOR COUPLES-CONVERSATION IDEAS THAT WILL SURPRISE YOUR

Here is another Guest Post by Kat. In today's article, Kat shares her thoughts on "Conversation Starters For Couples". She also referenced her personal experience. Please enjoy the article.

So you want to know some conversation starters for couples. It's an appropriate topic for people of any age in a relationship. It also doesn't matter where you are in the relationship. Whether you're dating someone seriously for the first time, jumping back into the dating scene, or you simply want to freshen up a long-term thing that needs some revitalization. No matter what your situation, it never hurts to ask questions that provoke deep, thoughtful discussions that will forge a new bond even deeper, or return the spark to an existing marriage.

First off, here's a hint: when it comes to conversation starters for couples and you're engaging in this kind of thing with your honey, turn off the tech. Unless you have no personal stereo and you use your computer or phone for music, that is. In which case, make sure all social media notifications are off. Trust me, those emails and social media posts can take a number and wait.

Better yet, go to a park with hiking trails and walk among the trees and birds while you commune with your sweetie. Besides, who doesn't love interspersing a deep conversation with kisses by a pond or a tree, especially if the conversation turns romantic, and maybe seriously spicy? And we know what that can lead to, right?

Conversation Starters For Couples-For Those Just Starting/Or Restarting Their Relationship

All right, so you're on the dating scene for the first time, or you're beginning the process again after a breakup. Either way, you've got a serious case of the butterflies, and you're bemoaning that 'just be yourself' advice because you want to make a good impression, right? Yeah, I thought so.

That is where conversation starters for couples can lend a hand. And they can range from the innocent to the saucy, depending on where you are in the relationship process. I would start with the innocent questions first, just because too many super-intimate details right out of the gate just feels awkward. But then, that's me.

My ideal questions are likely related to music and books because that's an area I feel comfortable with, such as:

"Which musician do you like best, and why?"

"Who's your favorite author?"

You could also ask questions like:

"Do you like animals? If so, what kind, and why?"

"Do you play video games? If so, which ones?"

"What's your favorite movie genre? Of that genre, what's your favorite movie?"

And on the list can go, at least in the "innocent" category. Once you've dated a specific person a while, and you're on the train headed real quickly for "Seriousville", you can ask the spicier conversation starters for couples that could not only lead to a deep discussion but an evening sans clothing, if that's where you both know you want to take things.

Such conversation starters for couples might include:

"What's the most romantic kiss you've ever experienced?"

"What's the most romantic gesture you've ever received?"

"Where do you like to be kissed the most?"

"What's your most favorite place to go to be intimate with some-one?"

"What's the most seductive music you've ever heard?"

You get the idea. I know, there are only five questions, but some-times it only takes a few questions to get the conversation rolling in a certain direction. Of course, you may want to save such questions for when the pair of you are alone or can get to a private place quickly if you're in a public place and things turn heated.

Conversation Starters For Couples-For Deeper Connection

Okay, so now you're in a committed relationship already and married or not, you're living together and you want to keep that connection going. Likely, you have at least six to ten common interests, and those alone can be good kindling for a discussion.

But we are all individuals with unique desires and goals, and pursuing those goals can be enriching for your relationship. We need to take time out though, to keep our partners in the loop of what we're doing, and perhaps to get deeper insight as to who they are, how they tick on a level even they might not have gone to yet. Conversation starters for couples in this stage might be:

"What do you think about planting a garden? What would you most like to plant?"

"If you could pick any place to have a vacation, where would it be?"

"If we were to have kids, what would your first choices for names be?"

"If one of us got relocated in our job, would you rather live in a city, or commute from a smaller town?"

Naturally, though, you want to do things together as a couple, and that can certainly be part of the discussions you might have. Perhaps you can learn something together, and that can fuel some really good conversations, plus you learn about each other in the process.

Conversation Starters For Couples-For Rekindling the Flame

But what if you're perhaps two or so decades into a relationship? Perhaps work and raising kids have left you a bit distant from your spouse, but you don't want to give up on what is otherwise a good thing.

There's still love there, but the flame's died down. You don't like that. Again, it helps to have mutual interests, but people grow and change over time, and the more time you spend apart from your partner, even due to work and kids, you and your spouse will need to spend some time rediscovering each other all over again. Date Night, Act 2—and conversation starters for couples to the rescue!

Possible conversation starters for couples:

"Let's try that new Italian restaurant and see how they prepare our favorites!"
"You know, in all the years we've been together, we've never done (fill in the blank)..."

"If we remodeled the kitchen, what would you want to have in it?"

"What do you think about taking up (fill in the blank)?"

From the beginning of a relationship to one's later years, these starters are just the beginning. Have fun finding new ones!

HEALTHY RELATIONSHIP QUIZ

So, you're in a relationship, and it's going ok, but some questions have come up and you're wondering if this relationship is healthy. A healthy relationship quiz will help you make sense of these questions and let you know just how healthy or unhealthy your relationship is.

A healthy relationship is never perfect, but some circumstances should not happen. Use this article like a healthy relationship quiz and take a hard look at your current relationship.

But before I dive into the healthy relationship quiz; there are several unwritten rules that you should be able to maintain in your relationship, whether you are married or in a relationship and plan to do so in the future.

Both Spouses Have The right to Speak Their Mind

You shouldn't set out to argue with your significant other when you find something you disagree on. There is a time and a place to be sensitive, or silent. That being said, parties in a healthy relationship should never feel they can't say what's really on their mind because their partner will be offended.

There is much that can be said about 'speaking the truth in love'. You are in a relationship because you love each other. If you love each other, you need to be willing to say hard things to strengthen each other.

If you are constantly guarding your tongue for fear your partner won't love you any more if you say what truly needs to be said, you are on dangerous ground. If you are afraid to say what you're thinking, your relationship is not healthy, and could even be bordering on abuse.

If you are in this scenario, try to figure out why you are afraid to speak your mind. Are you afraid your partner will get angry? Does your partner shame you by saying they were hurt by your words? If you are afraid to say something for fear of your partner's reaction, you should take a hard look at your relationship. If you can't communicate, your relationship probably won't last long.

You Should Feel Safe with Your Partner

When you are with your partner, you should feel like they have your best interests in mind. If you find yourself second-guessing yourself, or wondering if they still like you, you may want to rethink your relationship.

You should also never feel put down or scared they might hurt you. Everyone makes mistakes, so don't end a relationship just because your partner said one unkind thing, but be concerned if unkind words or actions become frequent, or if you become afraid for your safety. A healthy relationship is built on mutual respect. A partner should never force you to do something you are uncomfortable with.

Many people in dating relationships, especially females, have ended up being abused because their partner told them something to the effect of 'if you loved me you would...'. You are in control of your own body, and your actions. If you don't feel comfortable doing something, it's okay to say no. If your partner won't take 'no' for an answer, your relationship could be borderline abusive and you may need to go through the healthy relationship quiz to find out whether this is a healthy relationship or not.

You Are Both Free to Have Other Friends

There is nothing wrong with an exclusive relationship. This is a sign of a healthy relationship. If you have started to date seriously, you should treat this as a solid commitment unless something happens to change this.

The problem comes when you find yourself spending every spare moment with your significant other, and neglecting all your other friends. In the exciting early stages of a relationship, you might not be able to help yourself. But as things progress, you need to remember that other friendships are still important. You don't want to get in a situation where your partner starts to become jealous and sends you on a guilt trip every time you want to go out with your friends.

If this happens, have a serious conversation with your partner. Explain that you still love them, but want to spend time with your other friends. Assure them that it's not because you don't want to spend time with them, but that you need close friends to keep you strong. Good friendships outside your relationship will help you become a better person, which will improve your romantic relationship.

If your partner has concerns about the friends you are hanging around with, take the time to listen to their concerns. Maybe they are afraid you are going to cheat on them, or maybe they are genuinely concerned for your safety while you are out with certain people, or going to certain places. You may find that their concerns are warranted and might want to adjust your nights on the town.

When you do go out with friends, always avoid being alone with someone of the opposite sex. This is just a recipe for trouble. If you are committed to your relationship, you need to do everything you can to preserve it.

The Right to Make Your Own Choices

Whether it's finances, clothing, jobs, or anything else, both partners in a relationship should feel that they can make their own decisions.

When a decision will impact both parties, it should be discussed openly before the decision is made. This is part of a healthy relationship because communication is important. The problem arises when one partner makes all the decisions, or when decisions are made without consulting the other partner or one partner controls everything the other does.

This type of issue is particularly common in the area of finances. Couples need to decide what, and when they will spend on certain items. They should plan their financial goals together and ideally plan a good budget.

When they plan the budget, they should plan for an 'allowance' for each person. Each person should be allowed to spend a certain amount of money on whatever they want, and not have to justify their purchases to the other person. Depending on their financial situation, this may be impossible for some couples, but often, even a small amount of your own money can be freeing.

The rule is that only the decided upon amount can be spent and that the other partner can't judge on whether the purchase was necessary. If she chooses to spend her allowance on a chocolate bar, that's her business.

Couples need to learn to fight fairly over important choices and let the other choices go. Personal preferences are just that, personal preferences. They may define an individual to some degree, but they don't define the couple. Learn to be gracious and accepting of your partner's quirks and preferences. If she prefers Italian food, and you prefer to enjoy a good steak, find a restaurant that serves both.

The Right to A Healthy Relationship

Everyone deserves to find someone to spend the rest of their life with. This is not something to approach lightly. Take your time when developing a relationship, and watch for red flags that mean something is not right.

And so, talking about red flags here is a healthy relationship quiz that can raise red flags in your relationship. You might want to go through these. You can go through them together or separately. Or you do it separately and then together later.

The following true or false questions will help you understand your relationship better.

1. Do you ever feel devalued by your partner?
True/False
2. Does your partner put you down in public?
True/False
3. Has your partner ever pressured you to do something physical that you were uncomfortable with?
True/False
4. Do you feel uncomfortable around your partner's family?
True/False
5. Do you ever think your partner is cheating on you?
True/False
6. Are you afraid to share your deepest fear or desire with your partner?
True/False
7. Have you been unable to agree on major decisions, like buying a house or having children? True/False
8. Are you overly irritated with your partner's quirky, or annoying habits, such as leaving clothes on the floor, or regularly being late to things?
True/False
9. Do you feel like you could date again right away if something were to happen to your partner? True/False
10. Do you feel obligated to spend one on one time with your partner, but no longer truly enjoy it? True/False
11. Do you dislike your partner's hobbies?
True/False
12. If you were stranded on a desert island, do you think you would survive longer without your partner?
True/False

13. Do you dread having physical intimacy with your partner?

True/False

14. Do your fights result in extreme yelling or violence?

True/False

15. Do you often think of your former, single life and wish you could return to it?

True/False

16. Do you often wonder what life would be like if you had a different partner?

True/False

17. If you have children, do you find yourself arguing with your partner in front of the children regularly?

True/False

18. Do you disagree on what hobbies your children should participate in?

True/False

19. Does your partner make you feel unattractive?

True/False

20. Do you have a lot of trouble agreeing on what movie to watch?

True/False

21. Do you often argue over how to share the housework?

True/False

22. When your partner does something that bothers you, are you afraid to calmly bring it to their attention and talk about it openly?

True/False

23. If you go out on a date, do you spend most of your time looking at your phone?

True/False

24. Do you find yourself thinking you'd be relieved if something happened to your partner? True/False

25. Are you often tempted to flirt with co-workers and other people you meet?

True/False

26. Would you be embarrassed if your partner knew the negative thoughts you had about them? True/False
27. Does your partner ever threaten to physically hurt, or even kill you?

True/False

28. Do your friends express concern about the state of your relationship?

True/False

29. Do you wish you'd never met your partner?

True/False

30. Does your partner often speak harshly to you and hurt your feelings?

True/False

If you answered mostly false, your relationship is probably on good footing, if you answered mostly true, it's time for either a hard conversation with your partner or a breakup! If your partner is physically or verbally mistreating you, you may be the victim of abuse.

A person doesn't have to physically hit you to be an abuser. Everyone has their bad days, but if your partner is consistently speaking to you inappropriately, by calling you names, or demeaning you or your children, you may be being verbally abused. If your partner is threatening you, or even physically hurting you, you are being abused.

You do not have to stand by and tolerate this type of behavior. If you recognize signs of abuse in your relationship, reach out to a trusted friend or family member, or professional. The path to recovery will be long and hard, but there is life at the end of the tunnel.

INTIMACY QUESTIONS FOR COUPLES

The following are 20 questions for couples who are thinking about getting married. With these; now would be a great time to review all of them in detail and get to know your partner even better.

1- How did you meet?

The way a couple meets is going to give some great insight into their personality, did they meet at a bar or through mutual friends or online? There is no right or wrong way to meet people but if they met at a bar it shows they are bigger risk-takers than those who were set up as blind dates by their friends.

2- How old are each of you?

This is one of the old 20 questions for couples that are usually asked early on. Age plays a big role since we want different things at different stages in our lives. So, if he is 40 and you are 20 the relationship may not last.

3- Do you want children?

Another good 20 questions for couples to know just how committed their partner plans to be. Though this doesn't show how committed one might be in normal circumstances it's a good place to start.

Children are important to some individuals and others not as much but either way, this is an important discussion to have at the start of the relationship before things become "real" otherwise it could lead to anger and disappointment.

4- What are your religious beliefs?

The majority of the people in the world have religious beliefs that emphasize both people in the relationship to be of the same faith. And with good reason too. But this is the 21st century, such thinking is being considered outdated but all the same; so take that into account.

5- How important is a religion to you?

To some people, religion is not important while others it is a matter of great importance, if you are relaxed and your partner is super religious it may lead to issues so keep that in mind.

6- Where do you want to live?

If you are from one city and your partner is from another either you, her, or both of you may want to relocate or live closer to your family but that can lead to challenges. The only way this can be properly addressed is by sitting down and working out a fair compromise where everyone is satisfied.

7- Are you ready to settle down?

If you want to settle down and your partner does not this has to be addressed right away or there will be a considerable amount of resentment between both of you. As part of the 20 questions for couples that need answers before they get serious with someone, this shouldn't be overlooked.

There is nothing wrong with wanting to settle down or not but both of you need to want the same thing if the relationship is going to work.

8- Do you love me?

This is a key question and the answer needs to flow naturally if you are saying "I love you" but your partner is not it could be a sign your relationship is developing at different rates and you should reassess things. Another good one among the 20 questions for couples.

9- Do you trust me?

Trust is essential in any relationship so if you ask the question and cannot honestly answer "yes" it shows there is work to be done.

10- If we won the lottery right now what would you do?

If your partner lists a series of activities that do not involve you then it shows they were not really into you. Most people say to pay off bills, help family and travel or go shopping with the person they love.

11- What do you like most about me?

Tricky 20 questions for couples to ask but don't shy away from it though. By finding out what your partner likes most you will know what they focus on and maybe work on enhancing it.

12- What would you like least about me?

This will let you know whether there are qualities that get on your partner's nerves and can work through them before these problems take a serious toll on the relationship.

13- Have you ever cheated on someone before or been cheated on?

If your partner has cheated on someone before there is no guarantee they will not do it again. If you or your partner were cheated on, they may develop trust issues so these are things that must be taken into consideration.

14- Are you financially stable?

Money can't buy love but money problems can quickly turn a loving couple into bitter enemies so it would be smart to address these financial problems right away.

15- What are your career goals in life?

Having goals in life is important and if you or your spouse does not have goals it could be a sign of complacency.

16- Are your parents still married?

While this is not a guarantee but if your parents or the parents of your partner are still together it shows the child was raised in a household where the marriage was/is taken seriously.

17- What was the longest relationship you ever had?

This shows the person can make a long-term commitment which is key to keep in mind when looking for someone to spend the rest of your life with.

18- Do you believe in gender roles or everyone is equal?

Some individuals believe the woman stays home while the man earns a living while others believe in inequality. Whichever you prefer be sure your partner feels the same way, there is nothing that hampers a relationship like forcing someone to do something they do not want to.

These 20 questions for couples will help you both build a relationship that is based on not just love but also friendship, understanding, compatibility, and hope for a better tomorrow.

By addressing these 20 questions for couples it should become abundantly clear whether this relationship is destined for success. We cannot guarantee success but after getting these questions answered; both you and your partner will know how to keep your relationship going.

COMPATIBILITY QUESTIONS FOR COUPLES

There are lots of questions to ask someone whom you would like to spend the rest of your life with. Or just have a long-term close relationship with. But most of the popular couple questions that get brought up in a relationship seem to be based on how romance affects the couple.

And while it is an important part of a romantic relationship, romance is only a part of the big equation. To know the real level of compatibility of any two people, four conditions need to be taken into consideration:

1- Knowing each other's past,

2- Having common ideas about dating,

3- Loving each other's personality and

4- Being aware of the intentions each person has for the relationship.

While all four of the above factors are important, if you or your significant other is not attracted to each other's personality – there is little to no point in continuing the relationship.

For this reason, the first parameter to think about is love and loving each other's personalities. You also need to be aware of the importance of love because some personal preferences (like religion or political views) can decide the fate of a relationship earlier than anything else

Couple Questions-Personality Questions

The hard truth is – some people are just not compatible. When someone is unwilling to compromise even a bit about a certain belief or an aspect of their way of life, they should rethink being together.

But, if you're both not too concerned with things like religion or politics, then you have a real chance and should focus on the details to find your connection. Asking each other the 8 **couple questions** that are detailed below can decide whether a couple has the potential for a long-term relationship.

Couple Questions-Religion

First off, if you don't consider religious beliefs to be paramount, but realize your partner is of a different religion, you'll have to ask these two basic **questions:**

1. Are you ready to compromise about your religious beliefs?

2. What do they entail in terms of lifestyle choices?

If the answer to the first of the above questions was positive, you can skip to the next one. However, if your significant other demands that you have the same faith as them, you're going to have to ask them about the basic principles of their religious beliefs.

If you just don't see yourself living up to the conditions they demand, be respectful to your partner's beliefs – explain why they would drastically affect your lifestyle.

A suggestion about religious relationships:
If you belong to a certain religion and are only interested in a partner with the same beliefs, you should look into specialized dating websites.

These are a potential resource for like-minded people who will be happy with a strong, serious relationship with you. The two most visited ones are:
Jdate.com *for Jewish people;*
Match.com *for Christians.*

Couple Questions-Politics

If, for example, your guy is the type to always involve politics in a conversation or if you're not a big fan of your woman's constant rants about "big brother", you should ask him/her these two questions:

3. How sure are you of your political beliefs?

4. Are they a principal, unchangeable thing for you?

You're in the clear if their first answer is uncertain and you may have a chance if their answer is "no" to the second one. But if your partner isn't budging on politics – you might want to stop there. Further involvement, in hopes that he will change, is likely a waste of both of your time.

Couple Questions-Psychological Issues

Below are a couple of questions to ask if you want to know whether your significant other has any strong psychological traits that may affect a relationship.

And also find out whether your partner is jealous, bi-polar, or is a "control freak". These can define the way you communicate with each other. So, if you aren't the extra-patient type, consider their response when you ask:

5. Are you a jealous person?

6. Have you ever been called a control freak?

Most jealous and controlling types of people will go to great lengths to deny having that flaw – which is your clue. Someone who hasn't been called jealous or described as a "control freak", won't have a reason to be frustrated at you for asking these **couple of questions**

7. Are you diagnosed with any slight disorder, like bi-polarity?

8. Do you feel depressed often?

You might not want to ask this if you think you'll come off as offensive and insensitive. But if you get the feeling that something is on their mind you must do.

Otherwise, you'll end up dating someone with many needs

you may not be ready to fulfill. If you truly want to go on dating this man/woman, you must be aware of the issues they are coping with.

Couple Questions-Romantic Questions

At the start of a new relationship, there are no worries, except having great times in the good company. Romance-related couple questions aren't meant to dig too deep into the intimate opinions a person holds.

They are for gauging how romantically inclined someone is and how engaged he or she is willing to be in dating. The best time to ask these seven dating couple questions is at a time when you're alone.

But a dinner-date is also good. Each of these may spin off into a separate in-depth conversation, so try to be sure you have ample private time before starting to discuss romantic Couple Questions-.

1. *Is having common factors important, or do you think opposites attract?*

2. *What do you think of when someone talks about a romantic date?*

3. *Do you believe in love at first sight? Do you believe in the "friend zone"?*

4. *Have you ever met a person who was just way too in love with someone? What did you think of them?*

5. *What about too much mutual love? What do you think of couples who can't get enough of each other?*

6. *Do you believe that two people could be dating and be each other's best friend at the same time?*

Couple Questions About Past Relationships

Some people say they believe everybody can change, but they still want to know about the past of anyone close to them. First of all, if someone has a record of cheating on their partner(s), there's likely a real chance that they will cheat on you too.

Meanwhile, some people require you to be constantly close by, but others need to be reminded that they're in a mutual romantic relationship every day.

These traits can create a lot of tension in a relationship. If you want someone who trusts you and respects your personal space, ask them how they feel about spending time apart.

All of these factors can be determined by learning about your partner's past, particularly their dating experiences. A lot of people who cheat or have trust issues tend to fall into the same habit.

Most of them are self-destructive, neurotic, or prone to violence as well. So, while some people deserve a second chance, and it's up to you whether to give them one, detecting it early on can signal the return of their pattern.

Ask them the four questions below and carefully consider their reaction.

1. *Have you ever cheated on someone?*

2. *Have you ever been cheated on?*

3. *Have you ever been in a co-dependent relationship?*

4. *How did you end your last relationship?*

If you would like to know more about Couple Questions, then

check out the links below and remember to leave some love.

CONVERSATION QUESTIONS FOR COUPLES

I always think that the most important ingredient in a relationship is communication. And to communicate, you need to talk. And talking starts with conversations and conversation questions for a couple is a great way to kick things off.

No matter how strong their connection is, there is bound to come a trying time for every couple. Most often, this occurs when the initial emotional intensity dies down and both partners feel like there isn't anything new in their relationship.

If you think that there's not much left for you to discover about your significant other, you're not alone. Most long-time partners can guess their partner's reaction to just about any situation. They know what to order each other when they go out to eat, they know the ending of every story their partner will tell at parties, and so on.

On the one hand, your relationship is comfortable because of how predictable it is, which can be a truly beautiful thing if you both value it. But on the other, you must now make a much greater effort to engage in interesting, in-depth conversations with each other. And it's very difficult, especially after spending an exhausting day at the office, for one partner to find the extra energy needed to exceed the other's expectations.

If you don't take the time to constantly develop and improve the level of engagement and connection in your relationship, your significant other might think you're disinterested. And if they think that way or worse – if they're sure that you have no interest in the romantic bond you share; how do you think they'll act toward you?

This cycle of disappointment is highly detrimental to even the strongest relationships. It can be the cause of countless problems that result in the loss of intimacy a couple once shared. And, ultimately, this can be followed by their break up.

The fact that simple miscommunication can cause this level of relationship problems must be alarming to you if you're in a similar situation. But, think about it. If a lack of communication is the root of the problem, how can you make sure you hold on to your relationship, improve the quality of intimacy and become more engaging with your partner?

Of course – you talk to him/her! So, what better way that than with the use of conversation questions for couples?

Remember how you used to gaze into each other's eyes and spend hours on end talking? If you feel disconnected, look at him or her and insist on having a meaningful conversation. Do this a few times and your partner is bound to show the same initiative soon enough.

These conversation questions for couples will eventually help you become more romantically connected than you've been in a very long time. That initial intensity that made you fall madly in love with each other can be reignited – all you need is the same level of conversation you once had.

Here are 20 of the best conversation questions for couples who want to reconnect:

1- If you won a million bucks, what is the first thing you'd buy?
Discuss what you would purchase for each other.

2-What's the one thing you would do if you weren't scared of trying it?

This is a perfect time to show you're engaged – just be honest.

3-What are the top three things you love most about me?
Your partner should write their answers down and you then guess what he/she wrote.

4-When was the last time you felt touched by someone's kindness or compassion?
Describe to them how your last good deed made you feel.

5-What was the first thing you thought of me?
Were you right? In what ways were you mistaken?

6-What would your dream vacation be like?
After you discuss your dream vacations, draw out a route path you can take to see both of your number one choices.

7-If you could pick just one person, who would you say is your hero?
Why? Which of these qualities does your partner exhibit?

8-What was the single most embarrassing thing you did in your life?
Which of you had it worse?

9-Is there a single event that changed your life and who you were?
Did you think the change was positive? Did it turn out to be?

10-What was the last time you felt "butterflies" in your stomach?
When did I give you that feeling last?

11-What do you consider the biggest difference between me and you?
How are we similar? Discuss how these character traits shaped your relationship.

12-What do you like seeing me wear at home? What about when we go out?
Talk about the clothes that went out of fashion since you met. Try to recall how you/we dressed when you/we saw each other for the

first time.

13-What do you think of when you hear the word "romantic"?
Would you be flattered if someone called you a romantic?
Take turns describing, step by step, your dream romantic night out.

14-Do you consider yourself a pessimist or an optimist?
Was there a time you would say the opposite? Why do you think you changed your point of view?

15-Do you have a phobia? Did you have one as a child?
What was your biggest fear when you were little?

16-Is there something that motivates you in life?
Can you explain how?

17-Do you think there's anyone deal-breaker, even if everything else is perfect about a person?
Did your opinion about this change throughout the past 5-10 years?

18-What was the best dream you ever had? Did you ever have nightmares?
Interpret your dreams based on what your life was like at the time.

19-What has changed for the worse since we started dating? What improved?
Provide a few examples each.

If you would like more about Conversation Questions for Couples, then check out the links below, and don't forget to show some love.

CONCLUSION

In conclusion, communication in marriage demands continuous effort and care. If something prevents both partners from communicating within a significant period, they will likely find it harder to do once they finally attempt to carry on.

If you neglect to communicate with your spouse, you´ll not only be losing practice, you´ll be letting unattended issues pile up as well and letting the emotional distance between both partners increase.

There is no doubt the importance of communication in marriage. For one thing, it improves your compatibility with each other. It will also create room for an honest atmosphere, laughter, and friendship.

The benefits are limitless You might just be saving your relationship you never know.

So, if there is one single, most important idea you should always bear in mind, regarding communication in marriage, it is to never stop practicing. Part of the questions for couples is asking how to improve and maintain the relationship, never stop asking those questions

MY GIFT TO YOU

Scan the QR-Code Below

Romantic Ideas for Couples